GET TO KNOW Finnigan

Published in 2011 by Stewart, Tabori & Chang
An imprint of ABRAMS

www.gettoknowbooks.com

ISBN: 978-1-58479-862-0

Editor: Jennifer Levesque
Designer: Alissa Faden
Production Manager: Tina Cameron

The text of this book was composed in Block Berthold and Caecilia.

Printed and bound in the U.S.A.
10 9 8 7 6 5 4 3 2 1

THE ART OF BOOKS SINCE 1949
115 West 18th Street
New York, NY 10011
www.abramsbooks.com

GET TO KNOW YOUR KID

Shana Connell Noyes

Stewart, Tabori & Chang

New York

FOREWORD

Parents and children live in a world consumed by play-dates, computers, and video games. The focus on socialization, technology, and achievement-oriented success leaves little time for personal connections and the deep bonds that they foster. Old traditions such as baby books and handwritten holiday cards are almost things of the past, having been replaced by online memory pages and baby Web sites. How, then, in this fast-paced world can we find the time to enjoy and celebrate our children, to really hear from them, to make them feel heard?

Get to Know Your Kid provides the opportunity to take a few steps back and enjoy what is right in front of us, without having to chase or acquire. It provides the time and structure for deep connection. The questions that make up the book have been selected as ideal for sparking an intimate dialogue. They are designed and appropriate for children from ages four to ten, and can be revisited from time to time as your child matures. Building the foundation for connection and trust between yourself and your child in these formative years will lead to stronger relationships during adolescence and beyond. Thus, multiple benefits come from the process of completing the pages of *Get to Know Your Kid*.

The book provides a wonderful way for parents to practice nonjudgmental, active listening—truly the most challenging of feats, but when achieved, the most meaningful. Active listening is more than just paying partial attention to the children while multitasking through a day. Parents must put their own needs on hold and focus attention on the needs of the child. One of the greatest contributions Carl Rogers made to the fields of psychology, psychiatry, and psychotherapy was identifying the value of active listening, the ability to "listen with interest, and appreciate without interruption." Recent studies suggest that the most successful parent training programs include a component of "training in emotional communication." While *Get to Know Your Kid* does not claim to be a self-help parent handbook, the book does promote this positive parenting skill.

Get to Know Your Kid is devised so that anyone can use it easily, but its design derives from clinical experience. The questions could be used while children are playing, eating, or swinging at the park. Many are used in child therapy to facilitate play or discussion about feelings and perceptions

of existence. Wherever you ask these questions, the objective is the same—to capture a moment in your child's life that may otherwise have been missed, and to foster healthy dialogue.

Get to Know Your Kid is a personal and valuable memento of childhood, a beautiful gift for a child. It not only serves as a precious keepsake, but it also deepens the relationship you share.

Emily Piper, PhD, Registered Psychologist
Children's and Women's Health Centre
Vancouver, British Columbia
Clinical Assistant Professor, Faculty of
   Medicine/Department of Psychiatry
University of British Columbia

Damon Elgie, PhD, Registered Psychologist
Team Leader, Child & Youth Mental Health
Ministry of Children & Family Development
Vancouver, British Columbia

INTRODUCTION

One night two years ago, I took my then eight-year-old son out to dinner, just us. After we ordered our meal, I asked my usual question, the one I ask every day: "How was school?" He answered me with his standard, one-word response—"Fine"—and then our table went quiet. As I sat looking at my son, I wanted so much to know what was going on with him. I wasn't sure he felt like talking, but I decided to try anyway. I began asking him different questions, open-ended and unusual questions unrelated to the pattern of his day. I asked him what his earliest memory was. I asked him to pick his favorite word. I asked him if he had to be an animal rather than a boy, what animal would he be? And I was astounded by his reaction.

Talkative and animated, he opened up. He was full of imagination, opinions, likes and dislikes, fears and hopes. "Ask me another question," he kept saying. I realized that he definitely felt like talking. All I had to do was ask questions that he wanted to answer. That night, I learned that my son's earliest memory is walking on a boat dock when he was a toddler and looking down at the water of Lake Tahoe between the planks. His favorite word is *why*. If he had to be an animal, he'd be a tiger.

"Why a tiger?" I had asked, expecting him to answer that tigers are ferocious and scary and powerful.

"Because I want to be like Hobbes," he had answered. "From my comic book *Calvin and Hobbes*. He's hilarious and fun, and he's such a loyal friend."

His answers amazed me. I learned more about my son in that one evening than I had in a very long time.

When we got home, I thought about our conversation and I knew that I wanted to remember all the remarkable things my son had said. I wanted to be able to look back, years from now, and remember how his mind worked at eight years old—what worried him, excited him, made him laugh. Hurriedly, I started scribbling down everything I could remember.

Talking that night had a real impact on both my son and me. My son kept up his "ask me another question" attitude, and I kept asking new questions. I started asking my five-year-old daughter questions and writing down her answers. Suddenly I realized that I had the beginnings of a book that every parent needs: a book of questions that helps you get to know one of the most important people you'll ever meet—your child.

We all want to remember our children's early years.

And as we all know, childhood goes by way too fast. Children change so much, so quickly, that it's easy to forget many of the important things that happen along the way. We try to find the time to keep up with baby books and write down the magical things our children say, but things get busy. The moments we want to preserve in memory pass and are forgotten.

Get to Know Your Kid will help you change that. It gives you a way to take a moment out of your busy life, sit down with your child, and really connect. Created with the guidance of two child psychologists, the questions that make up *Get to Know Your Kid* are specifically designed to foster communication and real understanding between you and your child. There are no right or wrong answers to the questions. There's no need for criticism or judgment. All you need to do is listen. When you want to know more, ask your child to elaborate. Ask why. As you ask the questions in *Get to Know Your Kid*, you will begin to see the amazing world inside your child's mind. Children are imaginative, astonishing, remarkable people who have so much to say if only given the chance.

Last week I was stuck in traffic with my daughter. I asked her how school went, got the requisite "fine," and then the car went quiet. Next I asked her a question from

Get to Know Your Kid—what animal she'd be if she weren't a girl. Even though it's not an animal, I was sure she'd answer "butterfly," because that's what she is—whimsical and sweet, delicate and free-spirited.

Without a moment's hesitation she replied, "I'd be a snake."

I was completely stunned, but I responded evenly, "Why a snake?"

"Because snakes have nothing to be afraid of," she answered.

"And where would you live?" I asked her.

"In a field," she answered.

"Why a field?" I asked.

"Lots of rabbits in a field, Mom," she answered. In the rearview mirror I saw her smiling like the cat who ate the canary.

These are the kind of everyday car rides that anyone can have with their kids, as you'll begin to see when you use *Get to Know Your Kid*. When you ask these questions, you'll start to see aspects of your child that you might never have known existed. Sometimes I've worried that my son is too ferocious and my daughter too meek. After asking them the animal question, I'm not so worried anymore.

The idea behind the book is simple: You talk to your kids by giving them questions that they actually want to answer. Within that simplicity, however, is so much. First, just sitting down, focusing on your child, and really listening to what she has to say is a powerful experience for her. Your child knows she is truly being heard. One question leads to another, and the dialogue you create will strengthen your relationship in such a positive and important way. As Dr. Piper and Dr. Elgie note in the foreword, this establishes a foundation of trust that fosters stronger relationships in years to come.

For parents, *Get to Know Your Kid* reminds us to take a moment out of our hectic lives and just enjoy our kids. Some of your child's answers will amaze you, make you laugh, or teach you something you hadn't known before. Some might show you ways to be a better parent.

Have fun with the questions. Ask as many as you want, wherever you like. They will prompt new conversations, whether you're at the dinner table, driving to school, sitting on an airplane, waiting in line at the store, or tucking your child into bed at night. The questions let you turn ordinary moments into extraordinary ones just by talking to your child.

Perhaps the best thing about *Get to Know Your Kid* is that with its pages complete, it is a memento like no other available today. It is better than any photograph or video could ever be, because it is the story of who your child really is, not just an image of what he looks like. The book lets you capture his magical thoughts—written in your own hand, in your child's own words. Together, the two of you create a handmade heirloom, one you will turn back to over and over in the years to come. *Get to Know Your Kid* lets you take one of the best times in your whole life and bottle it.

Enjoy making your own memories.

100
QUESTIONS
TO ASK
YOUR KID

DATE: March 21 2011

What do you like most about yourself?

I like my hair and how I am very funny.

What do you like best about our family?

I like how we sometimes hangout and watch a movie together.

How old are you today? How old do you feel?

I am 11 and I feel 45.

What was the
best day of your life?
Describe it.

The best day of my
life was my 7th

If someone you just met asked you to describe your parents, what would you say? How would you describe yourself?

What is your
earliest memory?
Describe everything you
can remember.

If you found a kitten
on your doorstep,
what would you do?

Do you worry about anything in particular? Do you worry about the future or are you excited about it?

DATE: _____

Do you think there is life on other planets? Why or why not? If your answer is yes, what do you think it's like there? If you could be an astronaut and go to outer space, would you?

Do you think you'll go to college someday? If so, what do you think it will be like? What would you like to learn about?

Would you say
your life is better
than most people's
lives or not
as good? Why?

Have you ever
been really scared
of something?

Do you think it's easier to be a boy or a girl? Why?

What is more
important to you—
money or happiness?
Health or happiness?
Why?

If you could go on vacation anywhere in the world for free, where would it be? Who would you take with you? How would you get there?

Do you like your name? Is there a name you think would suit you better? Do you have a nickname? What is your favorite name of all!

If you were an animal rather than a person, which animal would you be? Why? What do you think it would be like? Where would you live?

DATE:_____

Do you remember your dreams? Can you tell me about one of them?

If you could choose to be a genius at something, what would it be? Singing! Painting! Sports! Writing! Something else! Why?

Do you ever feel frustrated? When?

If you could change
one thing about
yourself, what would
it be? Why?

Do you think you'll have kids someday? How many? What do you think you'll name them?

Do you think in our family parents and kids spend too much time together, not enough time, or just the right amount? Do you have a favorite thing we do together as a family?

Is there anyone you'd like to trade lives with? Would you do it for a day or forever!

Would you like to be famous? If so, for what? What do you think it's like to be famous?

Draw a picture of yourself.

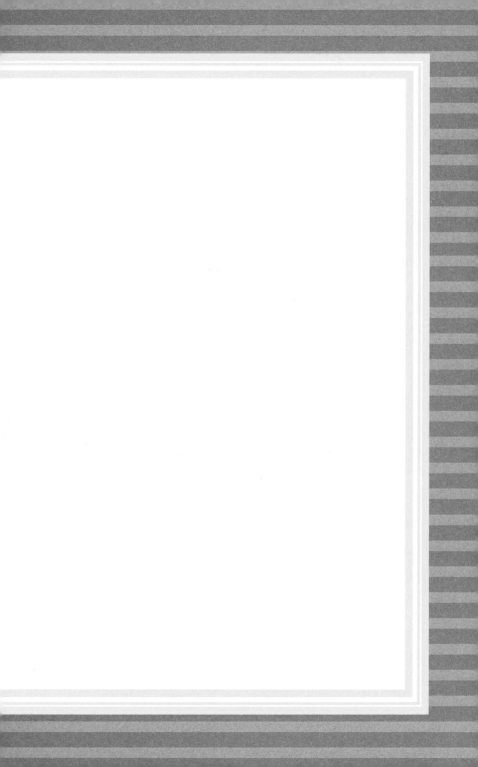

Are you jealous of anyone? Who? Do you think anyone is jealous of you? Why?

Are you excited to grow up! At what age do you start being a "grown-up"? At what age is somebody "old"?

What is your most
prized possession?
Where did you get it?
Why is it so special?
Would you ever sell it?
For how much?

Is there something you wish you could try but never have? What?

When you think about everything in your life, what are you most thankful for?

Do you have
any secret abilities
that no one
knows about?

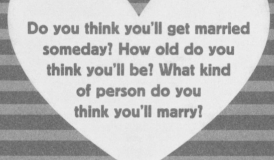

Do you think you'll get married someday? How old do you think you'll be? What kind of person do you think you'll marry?

DATE:

If you had a time machine, would you use it? Would you go to the future or the past? Would you stay there forever or just for a day?

What was the best part of your day today?

What is your favorite
book? Why? If you
wrote a book, what
would it be about?

If you had a crystal ball that could show your future, would you look inside it? What do you think you would see?

How do you feel about trying new things? Does it make you excited or nervous?

What do you think
is your greatest
accomplishment?
How hard was it for
you to achieve?

If you had three wishes, what would you wish for?

If you could give one of your wishes
away, would you? If so, who would get your wish?

DATE:

What is the hardest thing about being a kid? What is the best thing? Do you think it's easier to be a child or an adult?

What is your favorite animal? Would you like to own one? How would you take care of it?

Are you afraid of the dark? Why or why not?

Do you believe in luck? Do you have a good luck charm? If you could be either lucky or smart, which one would you choose?

Do you think dreams can come true? What about wishes?

Can you remember at all what it was like being a baby?

If you could invite anyone in the world, living or dead, real or imaginary, to come over and play at our house, who would it be? What would you do together?

If you invented a machine that could do anything in the world, what would you make it do? What would it look like?

Have you ever been to an amusement park or fair?

Can you remember your first visit? Do you like roller coasters, or do you prefer a more peaceful ride like a merry-go-round? Do you like cotton candy, or are you more of a popcorn person?

DATE: _____

What do you think it takes for someone to be happy in life? What makes you happy?

Describe a perfect day. Would you want to do it every day? Once a month? Once a year?

Do you ever talk to your dolls or stuffed animals or imaginary friend? What do you talk about?

Do you prefer your friends to be older or younger than you? Why? What's the difference between the two?

What is the nicest thing anyone has ever done for you? What's the nicest thing you've ever done for somebody else?

What are rainbows made of? Do you believe the story that there's a pot of gold at the end of a rainbow?

Do you have any ideas about what you want to be when you grow up? Who do you think has the best job in the world? Do you think you could have it?

Who is the funniest person you know? Can you tell me something that person does to make you laugh? Do you think you're funny? Why or why not?

Why do birds fly away when people come near them? Do you wish they would stay and play with you?

DATE:

When do you feel independent? Is there anything that you're glad you can do all by yourself, with no one helping you?

Do you ever feel lonely, or do you enjoy being by yourself?

If you could have
a superpower,
what would it be?
What would you use
it to do?

What makes you most proud of our family? What are you most proud of about yourself?

How do you
show people you
love them?

Do you like to win? How important is it to you? How do you feel about losing?

Can you ride
a tricycle? A bicycle?
Who taught you how to
ride? Can you remember
what it was like the
first time you rode it
on your own?

DATE:

Do you know what I do all day while you're at school? Do you think it's harder to have a job or go to school? Why?

What person do you enjoy being with most in the world? What person do you enjoy being with the least?

Do you ever feel shy? When?

What is your favorite game to play with your friends? What makes it so much fun?

Do you think the meals we have at home are good? What's your favorite thing we cook? Is there something you can cook all by yourself?

How do you feel about sharing your things with other people? Do you like it when people share with you?

What do you think it was like to live in our hometown 100 years ago?

What would you do without television or computers or video games?

DATE: _____

What is your favorite color? Favorite number? Favorite word? Favorite food?

If you won a million dollars, what would you buy first? Would you save any of the money? Would you give any away? If yes, how much? To whom!

When you grow up and have a job, do you think you'd rather make a lot of money, even if you don't really like your job, or enjoy your job and not make as much? Why!

How do you think
airplanes fly? Have you
ever ridden in one?
What was it like?

Do you think it
would be fun to travel
to another country?
If so, where would
you like to go?

If you made a time capsule to bury in your backyard that would be opened by someone in one hundred years, what would you put inside? What would those things tell people in the future about you and what your life is like today?

Have you ever made a really big mistake? What happened?

Have you ever had a
really good birthday?
How did you celebrate
it? Do you like cake or
the frosting better? How
would you make the
ultimate birthday cake?

DATE:

Who is your best friend?
What do you like
best about that person?
Is there anything you
don't like?

Have you ever done anything really brave? Tell me about it.

Do you have any habits, like biting your nails or cracking your knuckles? If so, could you break the habit if you tried? Would it be hard to stop? Why do you think people have habits?

Do you like having rules? Do you usually follow the rules? Why do you think we have rules?

Do you like learning new things? Is there anything you are excited to learn how to do?

What is the best thing about school this year? What is the worst?

Do you believe in magic?

Have you ever spotted a magical being, like a unicorn, a fairy, or a leprechaun?

DATE:

If you could give one person one gift and not have to pay for it, who would that person be and what gift would you choose?

Do you recycle paper and plastic? Why do you think people recycle?

If you could change one thing about the world, what would it be? Do you think the world will be a better or worse place in one hundred years? Why?

If you and I could change places for a day, what would you like me to experience of your life?
What would you like to experience of my life?

Draw a picture of yourself all grown up.

Is there something you'd like me to know about you that I don't know already?

Is there something you'd like to ask me?

What values are most important in our family? Are they important to you too?

What is your favorite place in the world? Why?

What is a hero? Is there anyone you consider your hero?

How do you feel today, right now, about your life?

ABOUT _____

My kid's name is: _____

He/She is _____ years old

We live at: _____

He/She is happy we made this book because: _____

_____

_____

_____

_____

His/Her favorite moment of making this book was:

_____

_____

_____

_____

For our next book, he/she would like to write about:

_____

_____

_____

_____

_____